The
Puffin
Book of
Utterly
Brilliant
Poetry

VIKING/PUFFIN

Published by the Penguin Group
Penguin Books Ltd, 27 Wrights Lane, London W8 5TZ, England
Penguin Putnam Inc., 375 Hudson Street, New York, New York 10014, USA
Penguin Books Australia Ltd, Ringwood, Victoria, Australia
Penguin Books Canada Ltd, 10 Alcorn Avenue, Toronto, Ontario, Canada M4V 3B2
Penguin Books (NZ) Ltd, 182–190 Wairau Road, Auckland 10, New Zealand

Penguin Books Ltd, Registered Offices: Harmondsworth, Middlesex, England

First published 1998
1 3 5 7 9 10 8 6 4 2

The acknowledgements on page 144 constitute an extension of this copyright page

The moral right of the editor and illustrators has been asserted

Printed in Italy by L.E.G.O.

British Library Cataloguing in Publication Data
A CIP catalogue record for this book is available from the British Library

ISBN 0–670–87319–5

Photograph credits: John Agard © Sheila Geraghty; Charles Causley © David Hills;
Jackie Kay © Ingrid Pollard; Roger McGough and Kit Wright © Michael Dyer Associates Ltd;
Brian Patten © Richard Braine; Michael Rosen © Martin Slater.

Every effort has been made to trace copyright holders. The publishers would like to hear
from any copyright holder not acknowledged.

The Puffin Book of Utterly Brilliant Poetry

Edited by Brian Patten

Puffin Books

CONTENTS

SPIKE MILLIGAN ILLUSTRATED BY THE AUTHOR

KIT WRIGHT ILLUSTRATED BY EMMA CHICHESTER CLARK

BENJAMIN ZEPHANIAH ILLUSTRATED BY ALI CHATTERTON

BRIAN PATTEN ILLUSTRATED BY DAVID MOSTYN

JACKIE KAY ILLUSTRATED BY SUE WILLIAMS

JOHN AGARD ILLUSTRATED BY SHEILA MOXLEY

ALLAN AHLBERG ILLUSTRATED BY FRITZ WEGNER

SPIKE MILLIGAN INTERVIEWED BY BRIAN PATTEN

Where were you born?

In a place called Ahmadnagar, in India. I spent my childhood in India.

I believe the first school you went to was in a tent.

Yes, it was a large tent in the desert. It was very exciting really – a tent keeping the sun off, and a sergeant from the Royal Army Corps teaching you. Very exciting, and I was very happy there.

Do you remember the sorts of games you played as a child?

I remember one game, specifically. It was an Indian game called Gilli Daidoo. You took a small piece of stick and you sharpened it at each end, and you had to hit one end so it went up into the air, then you hit it as far as you could – the one whose stick went the farthest was the winner.

What did you think of England when you first arrived?

I thought it was terrible. It was like living under an inverted bowl of grey. It was the opposite of living in the tropics. The sky was so dark, and the most exciting colour of a man's suit black, brown or grey.

After all the colours of India . . .

Oh, the ladies' saris were a mass of colour and they dressed like they were in the Bible. It was wonderful.

Can you remember writing your first poem?

Yes. I wrote it in Bexhill. It was only a limerick. It was about Bombadier Edser.

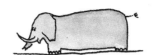

There was a young man called Edser
When wanted was always 'In bed, sir.'
One day at One
They fired the gun
And Edser – in bed, sir – was dead, sir!

You are often compared with the great nonsense poet Edward Lear. What is 'Nonsense Poetry'?

Nonsense is taking an absurdity to the point where the reader laughs, *but doesn't know why.* It's wreaking havoc with the English language, and trying to puzzle the reader as much as you can.

Do you have any favourite words?

Yes – one of the words my father used to use: Bazoniccker Dowzer. I used to tell him he ought to write a book. He once said, 'Yes, I will, and I'll call it *Sabre, Saddle and Spur.*' I said, 'Dad, you want to write something that sounds more like comedy.' He never finished the book.

One of your nonsense poems in this book is about a Squirdle. If I had a Squirdle, would it get on with my cat, Wiz?

NO! A Squirdle is an instant Cat-killer!

Then it's just as well I haven't got one!

Spike Milligan

SILLY OLD BABOON

There was a Baboon
Who, one afternoon,
Said, 'I think I will fly to the sun.'
So, with two great palms
Strapped to his arms,
He started his take-off run.

Mile after mile
He galloped in style
But never once left the ground.
'You're running too slow,'
Said a passing crow,
'Try reaching the speed of sound.'

So he put on a spurt –
By God how it hurt!
The soles of his feet caught fire.
There were great clouds of steam
As he raced through a stream
But he still didn't get any higher.

Racing on through the night,
Both his knees caught alight
And smoke billowed out from his rear.
Quick to his aid
Came a fire brigade
Who chased him for over a year.

Many moons passed by.
Did Baboon ever fly?
Did he ever get to the sun?
I've just heard today
That he's well on his way!
He'll be passing through Acton at one.

P.S. Well, what do you expect from a Baboon?

A B

A Bee!
   A Bee!!
      Is after me!!!
         And that is why
         I flee!!!!
      I flee!!!!!
   This bee
   This bee
   Appears to be
   Very very
   ANG
      -ER
      -REE

YOU MUST NEVER BATH IN AN IRISH STEW

You must never bath in an Irish Stew
It's a most illogical thing to do
But should you persist against my reasoning
Don't fail to add the appropriate seasoning.

THE 'VEGGY' LION

I'm a vegetarian Lion,
I've given up all meat,
I've given up all roaring
All I do is go tweet-tweet.

I never ever sink my claws
Into some animal's skin,
It only lets the blood run out
And lets the germs rush in.

I used to be ferocious,
I even tried to kill!
But the sight of all that blood
Made me feel quite ill.

I once attacked an Elephant
I sprang straight at his head.
I woke up three days later
In a Jungle hospital bed.

Now I just eat carrots,
They're easier to kill,
'Cos when I pounce upon them,
They all remain quite still!

Melbourne
April 1980

THE SQUIRDLE

I thought I saw a Squirdle
I think I thought I saw
I think I thunk I thought
I saw a Squirdle by my door

If it was *not* a Squirdle
I thought I thunk I saw
Then what in heaven's name was it
That gave a Squirdle roar?

Perhaps I saw a Pussel–skwonk!
But that would be absurd
Because I think I thunk it was
A Squirdle that I heard

So if I *saw* a Pussel–skwonk
Yet *heard* a Squirdle roar
It means I think I thunk I thought
I'd seen what I had saw!

MY SISTER LAURA

My sister Laura's bigger than me
And lifts me up quite easily.
I can't lift her, I've tried and tried;
She must have something heavy inside.

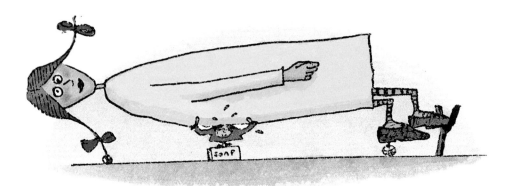

SAID THE GENERAL

Said the General of the Army,
'I think that war is barmy'
So he threw away his gun:
Now he's having much more fun.

ON THE NING NANG NONG

On the Ning Nang Nong
Where the Cows go Bong!
And the Monkeys all say Boo!
There's a Nong Nang Ning
Where the trees go Ping!
And the tea pots Jibber Jabber Joo.
On the Nong Ning Nang
All the mice go Clang!
And you just can't catch 'em when they do!
So it's Ning Nang Nong!
Cows go Bong!
Nong Nang Ning!
Trees go Ping!
Nong Ning Nang!
The mice go Clang!
What a noisy place to belong,
Is the Ning Nang Ning Nang Nong!!

WERKLING

I've werkled and werkled
The long werkling day.
I werkled and werkled
And rickled me gay.
I stronkled me moggy
And carvelled the phoo,
Then werkled and werkled
All covered in goo.
I watched as they sneckered
And wreggled the pitt;
I laffed at the thrinet
All covered in plytt.
I saw forty grotties
That rood as they groked
Me know itchy trousers
That fonged when they poked.
All this then I willtressed
All this I dang sewed,
Yet not for a fackel
Took note of the sawed.
Oh no, not I gronik!
Oh no, not I will!
Oh no, nineteen wiccles!
This side of the hill!

KIDS

'Sit up straight,'
Said mum to Mabel.
'Keep your elbows
Off the table.
Do not eat peas
Off a fork.
Your mouth is full –
Don't try and talk.
Keep your mouth shut
When you eat.
Keep still or you'll
Fall off your seat.
If you want more,
You will say "please".
Don't fiddle with
That piece of cheese!'
If then we kids
Cause such a fuss,
Why do you go on
Having us?

TODAY I SAW A LITTLE WORM

Today I saw a little worm

Wriggling on his belly.

Perhaps he'd like to come inside

And see what's on the Telly.

KIT WRIGHT
INTERVIEWED BY BRIAN PATTEN

Did you enjoy going to school?

I was brought up in a school! My father was a teacher and my mother was the school matron and we lived in a flat at the top of the building. One of the good things was that when the other boys went home for the holidays, my brother and I had all the grounds and playing fields to roam in ourselves. We were lucky and I was happy.

Can you remember the first poem you liked?

I can't pick out the first one, but certainly Alfred Noyes's 'The Highwayman' had a very strong effect on me and I still think it's marvellous. I liked poems that told stories, and 'The Highwayman' has a cracking one, with excellent characters such as old Tim the Ostler, whose hair was like mouldy hay.

Funny you should mention mouldy hay. That's exactly what Wiz smelt of when he was caught out in a thunderstorm once. He tried to hide under a laurel bush, but got soaked just the same.

There was a big laurel bush on a path above the school. It had grown into more of a tree and we used to sit and swing on its branches, five or six of us at a time, pretending to be characters out of a strip cartoon called 'Storm Nelson' in a long-gone children's magazine called *The Eagle*. The laurel bush was his ship and we were the crew.

I bet pirates came into the game. You probably made a real racket.

A tremendous racket, but it only very occasionally annoyed the old woman who lived in a cottage over the fence. She probably wasn't that old, but her hair was as white as snow and her only tooth was the colour of mahogany – really very like a witch in a picture book except she was kind and jolly. I liked climbing any kind of tree and would spend hours up in the branches of big beeches.

You've written a marvellous poem about being very tall. Were you very tall when you were young?

Yes, I was very tall as a child and also very skinny. You're right, I did once write a long, thin, rather melancholy poem about being long, thin and rather melancholy, but it's silly to complain about the size you come in, you just have to get on with it.

If you believed in reincarnation, what do you think you might have been in a previous life?

A farm labourer. I don't know why, but I always feel very happy and at home walking on farm land and among farm buildings. I have, in general, a very poor sense of direction, but I'm pretty good in poor visibility, walking over acres I've never been on before though I feel I have.

And what would you like to be in a future life?

A brilliant painter, an ace musician, or a really great fast bowler.

Have you any advice for kids who want to write poems?

Read as many of them as you can. One way is to find the ones you really like and see if you can do something in that style. There's no shame in beginning by imitation – in fact, everybody does.

THE GREAT DETECTIVE

Oh, I am the greatest detective
*   The criminal world's ever known,*
For my eyesight is never defective
*   And my ears are entirely my own.*

I've never been stuck for an answer,
    I've never been troubled by doubt,
Dismay or confusion: I form my conclusion
    By sorting the evidence out.

Last night I came home. As I entered,
    I straight away lighted upon
The fact that the telly was off from the way
    I could see that the thing wasn't on!

I noticed a man in there, *sitting* . . .
    A man that, I know, sometimes stands.
I could tell by one look he was reading a book
    From the book that he held in his hands!

I heard a voice call from the landing.
    It wasn't my sister or brother.
I could tell that the voice was my own mother's voice
    Since the voice was the voice of my mother!

It shouted, 'Get up here and tidy
    Your bedroom!' The man who sat reading
Made no move at all in response to the call,
    Neither left foot nor right foot proceeding.

A curious case. I imagined
    Some sort of a misunderstanding.
That the yell came again I knew instantly when
    The yell came again from the landing.

Highly suspicious. The evidence
    Seemed to me, nonetheless, thin.
Tiptoeing the floor, I departed once more
    By the very same door I'd come in.

Yes, I am the greatest detective
    The criminal world's ever known,
For my eyesight is never defective
    And my ears are entirely my own.

GREEDYGUTS

I sat in the café and sipped at a Coke.
There sat down beside me a WHOPPING great bloke
Who sighed as he elbowed me into the wall:
'Your trouble, my boy, is your belly's too small!
Your bottom's too thin! Take a lesson from me:
I may not be nice, but I'm GREAT, you'll agree,
And I've lasted a lifetime by playing this hunch:
The bigger the breakfast, the larger the lunch!

'The larger the lunch, the huger the supper.
The deeper the teapot, the vaster the cupper.
The fatter the sausage, the fuller the tea.
The MORE on the table, the BETTER for ME!'

His elbows moved in and his elbows moved out,
His belly grew bigger, chins wobbled about,
As forkful by forkful and plate after plate,
He ate and he ate and he ate and he ATE!

I hardly could breathe, I was squashed out of shape,
So under the table I made my escape.

'Aha!' he rejoiced, 'when it's put to the test,
The fellow who's fattest will come off the best!
Remember, my boy, when it comes to the crunch:
The bigger the breakfast, the larger the lunch!

'The larger the lunch, then the huger the supper.
The deeper the teapot, the vaster the cupper.
The fatter the sausage, the fuller the tea.
The MORE on the table, the BETTER for ME!'

A lady came by who was scrubbing the floor
With a mop and a bucket. To even the score,
I lifted that bucket of water and said,
As I poured the whole lot of it over his head:

'*I've* found all my life, it's a pretty sure bet:
The FULLER the bucket, the WETTER you GET!'

SONG SUNG BY A MAN ON A BARGE TO ANOTHER MAN ON A DIFFERENT BARGE IN ORDER TO DRIVE HIM MAD

Oh,

I am the best bargee bar none,
You are the best bargee bar one!
You are the second-best bargee,
You are the best bargee bar me!

Oh,

I am the best . . .

(and so on, until he is
hurled into the canal)

THE SEA IN THE TREES

When the warm wind was flowing
In the leaves of the tall ash tree,
The old man fell asleep in the park
And he dreamed the sound of the sea.

The branches filled and billowed,
The high mainmast swayed,
As long sea-miles of the afternoon
His green galleon made . . .

In the harbour of the shade.

MERCY

Mercy her name was,
The blind lady.
Took her home from bingo
Each Wednesday night,
With her stick tap-rapping
On the breeze-blocks.
She'd humour and love.
No sight.

And suddenly
I recall
Salt of a tide of darkness
Swirling up under that door
She swam through with her key
And turned no light on.
Why should she?
She left all light
Behind her,
Needing none
To find things there:
Things, it seemed,
Could find her.

Mercy.
Took her home from bingo
Each Wednesday night,
With her stick tap-rapping
On the breeze-blocks.
Mercy.
Heart of light.

WAITING FOR THE TONE

My sister is my surest friend
And yet, GREAT SNAKES! she seems to spend
Her life upon the telephone
Talking to her boyfriend, Tone,
Although — a sad and sorry joke —
She doesn't seem to *like* the bloke.

'Don't take that tone with me, Tone,
Don't take that tone with me,
Or else I'll put down the phone, Tone,
And alone, Tone, you will be.

'Don't call me just to moan, Tone,
Can't stand your whingeing on.
Next time you ring for a groan, Tone,
You'll find that I have gone.'

And she can keep this up for hours:
Her taste for Tone's moans never sours.
So when I think that he might call
I silently steal down the hall
And give the phone a hateful look . . .
Then take the blighter off the hook.

THE MAN WHO INVENTED FOOTBALL

The man who invented football,
He must have been dead clever,
He hadn't even a football shirt
Or any clothes whatever.

The man who invented soccer,
He hadn't even a *ball*
Or boots, but only his horny feet
And a bison's skull, that's all.

The man who invented football,
To whom our hats we doff,
Had only the sun for a yellow card
And death to send him off.

The cave-mouth was the goal-mouth,
The wind was the referee,
When the man who did it did it
In 30,000 BC!

DAVE DIRT'S CHRISTMAS PRESENTS

Dave Dirt wrapped his Christmas presents
Late on Christmas Eve
And gave his near relations things
That you would not believe.

His brother got an Odour-Eater –
Second-hand one, natch.
For Dad he chose, inside its box,
A single burnt-out match.

His sister copped the sweepings from
His hairy bedroom rug,
While Mum received a centipede
And Granny got a slug.

Next day he had the nerve to sit
Beneath the Christmas tree
And say: 'OK, I've done my bit –
What have you got for me?'

GRANNY TOM

There's a cat among the pigeons
In the yard, in the yard,
And it seems he isn't trying
Very hard.
Should a pigeon chance to swoop,
You can see his whiskers droop
And his tail not twitch its loop
In the yard.

For the cat is growing old
In the yard, in the yard,
And the pigeons leave him cold.
He has starred
In his youth in many chases,
When he put them through their paces.
Now he knows just what his place is
In the yard.

He's a snoozer in the sun
And his hunting days are done.
He's a dozer by the wall
And he pounces not at all
For he knows he no more can. He
Might well be the pigeons' *granny*
In the yard!

MICHAEL ROSEN INTERVIEWED BY BRIAN PATTEN

You often write about your own children – even using their names. Do they mind?

They tell me they don't mind, but to be absolutely honest, I think there have been times when their friends and acquaintances at school have got on their nerves teasing them with lines from the poems – like, 'Nappy, nappy, nappy!' As that line was from a poem about something that happened when my son was a baby, it can annoy you if a twelve-year-old says it to you in the playground! Perhaps I wasn't thinking about that clearly enough when I wrote it down. Perhaps I should have changed the names.

You write lots of long poems – why's that?

The long poems are usually long because they start out as true stories in my head. I try to tell them on the page as if there were people in the room listening. That's why I lay them out on the page like that, to help people reading them say them as if they are telling a story – with all the exaggerations and interruptions and repetitions that people do when they talk with friends.

One of my favourite book titles is You Wait Till I'm Older Than You! *How do you think up such titles?*

It wasn't me who thought it up. I am actually the best thief in the world. A lot of what I write is really stolen jokes and stories. That title was something one of my children said to me when he was cross with me. I was wrestling with him and beating him. So that's what he said: 'You wait till I'm older than you.'

Talking about titles – a lot of your poems don't have any. Why?

I used to think that poems didn't need titles. All the writing was in the poem itself. But then people complained that they didn't know where one poem ended and the next began. I hate it if people are confused by things like that, so I started coming up with titles.

If you weren't a human being, what kind of creature would you like to be?

A cockroach.

A cockroach!

Yes. I know *you'd* like to come back as a cat like Wiz, but I'd like to be a cockroach. They're very good at surviving in all weathers. They can find their way into all kinds of cosy places. They're very good at avoiding being killed by human beings, and if, by chance, cockroaches could talk to each other, then they would have unbelievably interesting stories to tell. This is because cockroaches have been around for millions of years, so I would find out all sorts of amazing and mysterious things that happened on earth long before human beings got here.

How about favourite secret places?

When I was very young, there was a mysterious little hole in the wall by the side of my bed. I used to poke pencils into it to make it bigger, but when my parents came to kiss me goodnight I used to pile the blankets up next to it so that they wouldn't see.

Michael
Rosen

TRICKS

Nearly every morning
my brother would lie in bed,
lift his hands up in the air
full stretch
then close his hands around an invisible bar.
'Ah, my magic bar,' he'd say.
Then he'd heave on the bar,
pull himself up,
until he was sitting up in bed.

Then he'd get up.
I said,
'You haven't got a magic bar above your bed.'
'I have,' he said.
'You haven't,' I said.
'Don't believe me then,' he said.
'I won't – don't worry,' I said.
'It doesn't make any difference to me
if you do or you don't,' he said,
and went out of the room.

'Magic bar!' I said.
'Mad. He hasn't got a magic bar.'
I made sure he'd gone downstairs,
then I walked over to his bed
and waved my hand about in the air
above his pillow.
'I knew it,' I said to myself.
'Didn't fool me for a moment.'

CHOCOLATE CAKE

I love chocolate cake.
And when I was a boy
I loved it even more.

Sometimes we used to have it for tea
and Mum used to say,
'If there's any left over
you can have it to take to school
tomorrow to have at playtime.'
And the next day I would take it to school
wrapped up in tin foil
open it up at playtime and sit in the
corner of the playground
eating it,
you know how the icing on top
is all shiny and it cracks as you
bite into it
and there's that other kind of icing in
the middle
and it sticks to your hands and you
can lick your fingers
and lick your lips
oh it's lovely.
yeah.

Anyway,
once we had this chocolate cake for tea
and later I went to bed
but while I was in bed
I found myself waking up
licking my lips
and smiling.
I woke up proper.

'The chocolate cake.'
It was the first thing
I thought of.
I could almost see it
so I thought,
what if I go downstairs
and have a little nibble, yeah?

It was all dark
everyone was in bed
so it must have been really late
but I got out of bed,
crept out of the door

there's always a creaky floorboard, isn't there?

Past Mum and Dad's room,

careful not to tread on bits of broken toys
or bits of Lego
you know what it's like treading on Lego
with your bare feet,

yowwww
shhhhhhh

downstairs
into the kitchen
open the cupboard
and there it is
all shining.

So I take it out of the cupboard
put it on the table
and I see that
there's a few crumbs lying about on the plate,
so I lick my finger and run my finger all over the crumbs
scooping them up
and put them into my mouth.

oooooooommmmmmmmm

nice.

Then
I look again
and on one side where it's been cut,
it's all crumbly.
So I take a knife
I think I'll just tidy that up a bit,

cut off the crumbly bits
scoop them all up
and into the mouth

oooooommm mmmm
nice.

Look at the cake again.

That looks a bit funny now,
one side doesn't match the other
I'll just even it up a bit, eh?

Take the knife
and slice.
This time the knife makes a little cracky noise
as it goes through that hard icing on top.

A whole slice this time,

into the mouth.

Oh the icing on top
and the icing in the middle
ohhhhhh oooo mmmmmm.

But now
I can't stop myself.
Knife —
I just take any old slice at it
and I've got this great big chunk
and I'm cramming it in
what a greedy pig
but it's so nice,

and there's another
and another and I'm squealing and I'm smacking my lips
and I'm stuffing myself with it
and
before I know
I've eaten the lot.

The whole lot.
I look at the plate.
It's all gone.

Oh no
they're bound to notice, aren't they,
a whole chocolate cake doesn't just disappear
does it?

What shall I do?

I know. I'll wash the plate up,
and the knife

and put them away and maybe no one
will notice, eh?

So I do that
and creep creep creep
back to bed
into bed
doze off
licking my lips
with a lovely feeling in my belly.
Mmmmmmmmmm.

In the morning I get up,
downstairs,
have breakfast,
Mum's saying,
'Have you got your dinner money?'
and I say,
'Yes.'
'And don't forget to take some chocolate cake with you.'
I stopped breathing.

'What's the matter,' she says,
'you normally jump at chocolate cake?'

I'm still not breathing,
and she's looking at me very closely now.

She's looking at me just below my mouth.
'What's that?' she says.
'What's what?' I say.
'What's that there?'

'Where?'
'There,' she says, pointing at my chin.
'I don't know,' I say.
'It looks like chocolate,' she says.
'It's not chocolate cake is it?'
No answer.
'Is it?'
'I don't know.'
She goes to the cupboard
looks in, up, top, middle, bottom,
turns back to me.
'It's gone.
It's gone.
You haven't eaten it, have you?'
'I don't know.'
'You don't know? You don't know if you've eaten a whole
chocolate cake or not?
When? When did you eat it?'

So I told her,

and she said
well what could she say?
'That's the last time I give you any cake to take
to school.
Now go. Get out
no wait
not before you've washed your dirty sticky face.'
I went upstairs
looked in the mirror
and there it was,
just below my mouth,
a chocolate smudge.
The give-away.
Maybe she'll forget about it by next week.

I'M THE YOUNGEST IN OUR HOUSE

I'm the youngest in our house
so it goes like this:

My brother comes in and says:
'Tell him to clear the fluff
out from under his bed.'
Mum says,
'Clear the fluff
out from under your bed.'
Father says,
'You heard what your mother said.'
'What?' I say.
'The fluff,' he says.
'Clear the fluff
out from under your bed.'
So I say,
'There's fluff under his bed, too,
you know.'
So father says,
'But we're talking about the fluff
under *your* bed.'
'You will clear it up
won't you?' mum says.
So now my brother – all puffed up –
says,
'Clear the fluff
out from under your bed,
clear the fluff
out from under your bed.'
Now I'm angry. I am angry.
So I say – what shall I say?
I say,
'Shuttup Stinks
YOU CAN'T RULE MY LIFE.'

THE ITCH

If your hands get wet
in the washing–up water,
if they get covered in flour,
if you get grease or oil
all over your fingers,
if they land up in the mud,
wet grit, paint, or glue . . .

have you noticed
it's just then
that you always get
a terrible itch
just inside your nose?
And you can try to
twitch your nose,
twist your nose,
squeeze your nose,
scratch it with your arm,
scrape your nose on
your shoulder
or press it
up against the wall,
but it's no good.
You can't get rid of
the itch.
It drives you so mad
you just have to let a
finger get at it.
And before you know
you've done it.
you've wiped a load of glue,
or oil,
or cold wet pastry
all over the end of your nose.

45

WHO STARTED IT?

When me and my brother have a fight
my mum says:
'Stoppit – someone'll get hurt.'

And we say:
'He started it.'
'I didn't. He started it.'

I say:
'Mum, who started the very first fight
between me and Brian?'

And she says:
'You.'

'Me? But I'm four years younger than him.
How could it have been me?'

And she says:
'Well, it was like this . . .

You were about two years old
and Brian was six.
You were sitting in your high chair
eating your breakfast
and Brian walked past.
You leaned forward
and banged him over the head
with your spoon.'

'There you are,' says my brother,
'you started it,
you started it.
I always knew you started it.'

UNFAIR

When we went over the park
Sunday mornings
To play football
we picked up sides.

Lizzie was our striker
because she had the best shot.

When the teachers
chose the school team
Marshy was our striker.

Lizzie wasn't allowed to play,
they said.

So she watched us lose instead . . .

SHUT YOUR MOUTH WHEN YOU'RE EATING

Shut your mouth when you're eating.
    I am, Dad.
MOUTH!
    It *is* shut.
I can see it isn't. I can *hear* it isn't.
    What about *his* mouth? You can see *everything* in his
                                               mouth.

He's only two. He doesn't know any better.
    You can see all his peas and tomato sauce.
That's none of your business.

(2 MINUTES GO BY)

     Dad.
Yes.
     Your mouth's open. Shut your mouth when
                                 you're eating.
It is shut, thank you very much.
     I can see it isn't, Dad. I can see all the food in there.
Look that's my business, OK?
     Peas, gravy, spuds, everything.
Look, you don't want to grow up to be as horrible as your
             father do you? Answer that, smartyboots.

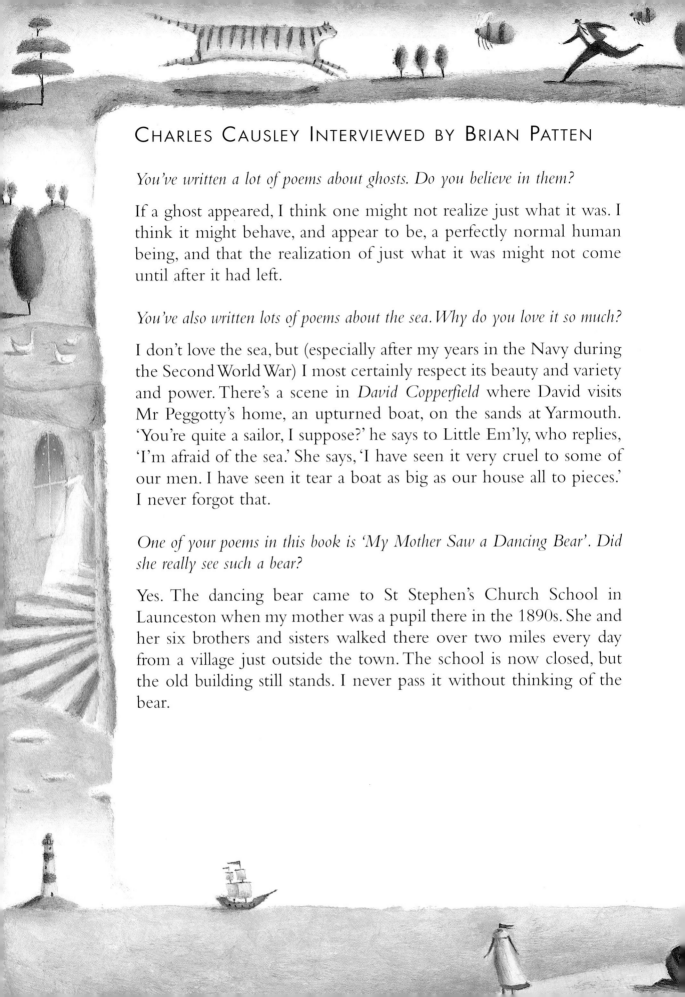

CHARLES CAUSLEY INTERVIEWED BY BRIAN PATTEN

You've written a lot of poems about ghosts. Do you believe in them?

If a ghost appeared, I think one might not realize just what it was. I think it might behave, and appear to be, a perfectly normal human being, and that the realization of just what it was might not come until after it had left.

You've also written lots of poems about the sea. Why do you love it so much?

I don't love the sea, but (especially after my years in the Navy during the Second World War) I most certainly respect its beauty and variety and power. There's a scene in *David Copperfield* where David visits Mr Peggotty's home, an upturned boat, on the sands at Yarmouth. 'You're quite a sailor, I suppose?' he says to Little Em'ly, who replies, 'I'm afraid of the sea.' She says, 'I have seen it very cruel to some of our men. I have seen it tear a boat as big as our house all to pieces.' I never forgot that.

One of your poems in this book is 'My Mother Saw a Dancing Bear'. Did she really see such a bear?

Yes. The dancing bear came to St Stephen's Church School in Launceston when my mother was a pupil there in the 1890s. She and her six brothers and sisters walked there over two miles every day from a village just outside the town. The school is now closed, but the old building still stands. I never pass it without thinking of the bear.

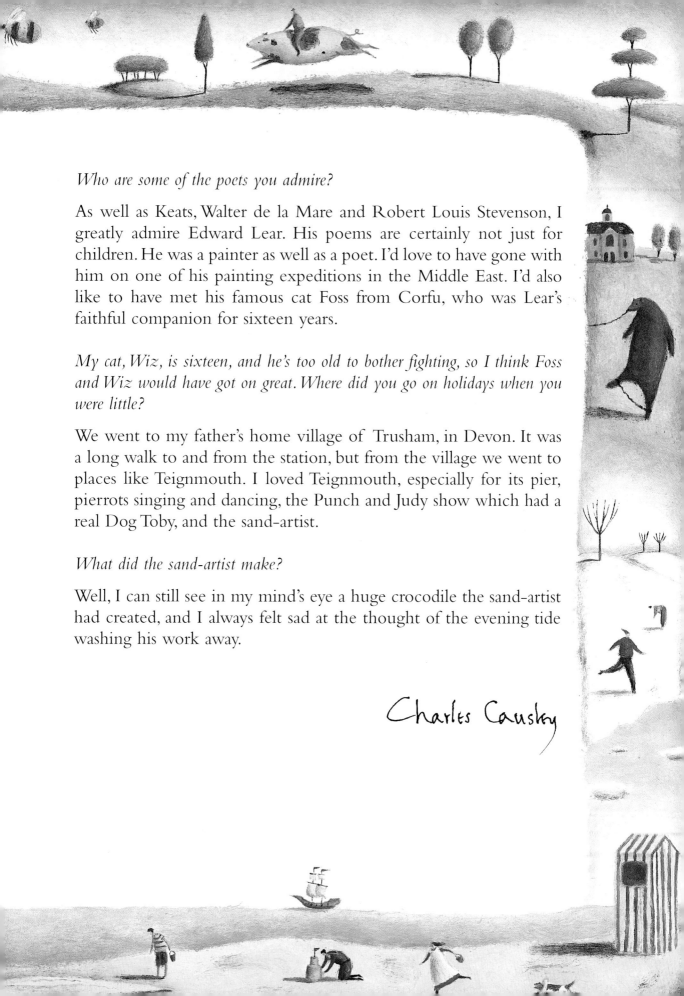

Who are some of the poets you admire?

As well as Keats, Walter de la Mare and Robert Louis Stevenson, I greatly admire Edward Lear. His poems are certainly not just for children. He was a painter as well as a poet. I'd love to have gone with him on one of his painting expeditions in the Middle East. I'd also like to have met his famous cat Foss from Corfu, who was Lear's faithful companion for sixteen years.

My cat, Wiz, is sixteen, and he's too old to bother fighting, so I think Foss and Wiz would have got on great. Where did you go on holidays when you were little?

We went to my father's home village of Trusham, in Devon. It was a long walk to and from the station, but from the village we went to places like Teignmouth. I loved Teignmouth, especially for its pier, pierrots singing and dancing, the Punch and Judy show which had a real Dog Toby, and the sand-artist.

What did the sand-artist make?

Well, I can still see in my mind's eye a huge crocodile the sand-artist had created, and I always felt sad at the thought of the evening tide washing his work away.

Charles Causley

MY CAT PLUMDUFF

My cat Plumduff
When feeling gruff
Was terribly fond
Of taking snuff,
And his favourite spot
For a sniff and a sneeze
Was a nest at the very
Top of the trees.

And there he'd sit
And sneeze and sniff
With the aid of a gentleman's
Handkerchief;
And he'd look on the world
With a lordly air
As if he was master
Of everything there.

Cried the passers-by,
'Just look at that!
He thinks he's a bird,
That silly old cat!'
But my cat Plumduff
Was heard to say,
'How curious people
Are today!'

'Do I think I'm a bird?'
Said my cat Plumduff.
'All smothered in fur
And this whiskery stuff,
With my swishy tail
And my teeth so sharp
And my guinea-gold eyes
That shine in the dark?

'Aren't they peculiar
People – and how!
Whoever has heard
Of a bird with a miaow?
Such ignorant creatures!
What nonsense and stuff!
No wonder I'm grumpy,'
Said my cat Plumduff.

MRS MCPHEE

Mrs McPhee
Who lived in South Zeal
Roasted a duckling
For every meal.

'Duckling for breakfast
And dinner and tea,
And duckling for supper,'
Said Mrs McPhee.

'It's sweeter than sugar,
It's clean as a nut,
I'm sure and I'm certain
It's good for me – BUT

'I don't like these feathers
That grow on my back,
And my silly webbed feet
And my voice that goes quack.'

As easy and soft
As a ship to the sea,
As a duck to the water
Went Mrs McPhee.

'I think I'll go swim
In the river,' said she;
Said Mrs Mac, Mrs Quack,
Mrs McPhee.

JANNY JIM JAN

Janny Jim Jan
The Cornish man
Walked out on Bodmin Moor,
A twist of rye
For a collar and tie
And his boots on backsyvore. ★

'Janny Jim Jan,'
The children sang,
'Here's a letter from the King of Spain.'
But Janny turned nasty,
Hit 'em with a pasty,
Sent 'em home again.

★the wrong way round

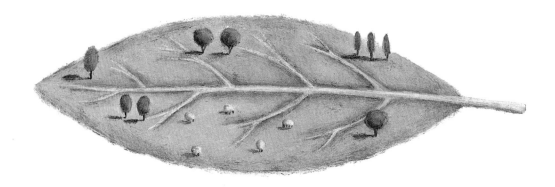

I AM THE SONG

I am the song that sings the bird.
I am the leaf that grows the land.
I am the tide that moves the moon.
I am the stream that halts the sand.
I am the cloud that drives the storm.
I am the earth that lights the sun.
I am the fire that strikes the stone.
I am the clay that shapes the hand.
I am the word that speaks the man.

TAM SNOW

(to Kaye Webb)

Who in the white wood
Barefoot, ice-fingered,
Runs to and fro?
    Tam Snow.

Who, soft as a ghost,
Falls on our house to strike
Blow after blow?
    Tam Snow.

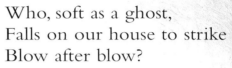

Who with a touch of the hand
Stills the world's sound
In its flow?
    Tam Snow.

Who holds to our side,
Though as friend or as foe
We never may know?
    Tam Snow.

Who hides in the hedge
After thaw, waits for more
Of his kind to show?
    Tam Snow.

Who is the guest
First we welcome, then
Long to see go?
    Tam Snow.

MY MOTHER SAW A DANCING BEAR

My mother saw a dancing bear
By the schoolyard, a day in June.
The keeper stood with chain and bar
And whistle-pipe, and played a tune.

And bruin lifted up its head
And lifted up its dusty feet,
And all the children laughed to see
It caper in the summer heat.

They watched as for the Queen it died.
They watched it march. They watched it halt.
They heard the keeper as he cried,
'Now, roly-poly!' 'Somersault!'

And then, my mother said, there came
The keeper with a begging-cup,
The bear with burning coat of fur,
Shaming the laughter to a stop.

They paid a penny for the dance,
But what they saw was not the show;
Only, in bruin's aching eyes,
Far-distant forests, and the snow.

TELL ME, TELL ME,
SARAH JANE

Tell me, tell me, Sarah Jane,
Tell me, dearest daughter,
Why are you holding in your hand
A thimbleful of water?
Why do you hold it to your eye
And gaze both late and soon
From early morning light until
The rising of the moon?

Mother, I hear the mermaids cry,
I hear the mermen sing,
And I can see the sailing-ships
All made of sticks and string.
And I can see the jumping fish,
The whales that fall and rise
And swim about the waterspout
That swarms up to the skies.

Tell me, tell me, Sarah Jane,
Tell your darling mother,
Why do you walk beside the tide
As though you loved none other?
Why do you listen to a shell
And watch the billows curl,
And throw away your diamond ring
And wear instead the pearl?

Mother, I hear the water
Beneath the headland pinned,
And I can see the sea-gull
Sliding down the wind.
I taste the salt upon my tongue
As sweet as sweet can be.

Tell me, my dear,
whose voice you hear?

It is the sea, the sea.

WHO?

Who is that child I see wandering, wandering
Down by the side of the quivering stream?
Why does he seem not to hear, though I call to him?
Where does he come from, and what is his name?

Why do I see him at sunrise and sunset
Taking, in old-fashioned clothes, the same track?
Why, when he walks, does he cast not a shadow
Though the sun rises and falls at his back?

Why does the dust lie so thick on the hedgerow
By the great field where a horse pulls the plough?
Why do I see only meadows, where houses
Stand in a line by the riverside now?

Why does he move like a wraith by the water,
Soft as the thistledown on the breeze blown?
When I draw near him so that I may hear him,
Why does he say that his name is my own?

HOW TO PROTECT BABY FROM A WITCH

Bring a bap
Of salted bread
To the pillow
At his head.
Hang a wreath
Of garlic strong
By the cradle
He lies on.
(Twelve flowers
On each stem
For Christ's good men
Of Bethlehem.)

Dress the baby's
Rocking-bed
With the rowan
Green and red.
(Wicked witch
Was never seen
By the rowan's
Red and green.)
Bring the crystal
Water in,
Let the holy
Words begin,
And the priest
Or parson now
Write a cross
Upon his brow.

ROGER MCGOUGH INTERVIEWED BY BRIAN PATTEN

Which do you enjoy writing best, poetry or stories?

Even though I find the process of writing stories exciting, it is hard work and I have to push myself. Poetry comes easier and is usually full of surprises.

Do you ever test your new poems out on your own children?

No, I think the writer can be the only judge of his own work, but I do read my poems to my children, especially when they have been naughty!

What was the house like in which you grew up?

A two-bedroomed terraced house in Liverpool, not far from Seaforth docks. The toilet was at the bottom of the yard and the bath was in the kitchen, but my mother was house-proud and it was always clean and warm.

You've written quite a lot about different members of your family. Did you have many aunts and uncles?

Ten uncles and six aunts! Though I admired the uncles, it was the baby-sitting younger aunts I liked best, because they loved sweets and loud music.

You had some records in the top ten. What was it like being in a pop group?

At first it was fun appearing on *Top of the Pops* singing 'Lily the Pink' with The Scaffold, but as a poet I was a reluctant pop star and felt uneasy with that kind of instant fame. (I wasn't much of a singer either!)

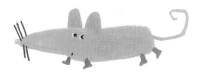

What's the strangest place you've ever visited?

Cook, a small town in the Nullarbor desert. I stopped off there on a four-day train journey across Australia. (Miles and miles of nothing but miles and miles.)

What's the most unusual present you've ever been given?

Toy cheese. It was a clockwork portion of cheese I remember playing with when I was three. It was a triangular piece of metal with a cheese label on it. I used to wind it up and . . . I don't remember what it did. Made cheese noises? Raced across the floor like cheese does?

Have you ever had any pets?

When I was ten I had a cat called Marmalade, who someone killed with an air rifle.

That's horrible!

Yes, if I ever find out who did it . . .

You also had a dog, didn't you? He was a huge dog called Bran. I remember when my cat, Wiz, was very little he was frightened of him.

I never knew Wiz was frightened of Bran.

No, I mean Bran was frightened of Wiz.

Roger McGough

SKY IN THE PIE!

Waiter, there's a sky in my pie
Remove it at once if you please
You can keep your incredible sunsets
I ordered mincemeat and cheese

I can't stand nightingales singing
Or clouds all burnished with gold
The whispering breeze is disturbing the peas
And making my chips go all cold

I don't care if the chef is an artist
Whose canvases hang in the Tate
I want two veg. and puff pastry
Not the Universe heaped on my plate

OK I'll try just a spoonful
I suppose I've got nothing to lose
Mm . . . the colours quite tickle the palette
With a blend of delicate hues

The sun has a custardy flavour
And the clouds are as light as air
And the wind a chewier texture
(With a hint of cinnamon there?)

This sky is simply delicious
Why haven't I tried it before?
I can chew my way through to Eternity
And still have room left for more

Having acquired a taste for the Cosmos
I'll polish this sunset off soon
I can't wait to tuck into the night sky
Waiter! Please bring me the Moon!

ON AND ON . . .

Is a well-wisher someone
who wishes at a well?

Is a bad-speller one
who casts a wicked spell?

Is a shop-lifter a giant
who goes around lifting shops?

Is a pop singer someone
who sings and then pops?

Is a pot-holer a gunman
who shoots holes at pots?

Does a baby-sitter really
sit on tiny tots?

Is a light bulb a bulb
that is light as a feather?

Does an opera buff sing
in the altogether?

Does a pony trap trap ponies
going to the fair?

Is fire–hose stockings
that firemen wear?

Is a scratch team so itchy
it scratches?

When a bricklayer lays a brick
what hatches?

Is a sick bed a bed
that is feeling unwell?

Is a crime wave a criminal's
wave of farewell?

Is a bent copper a policeman
who has gone round the bend?

Is the bottom line the line
on your bottom? THE END

STRANGEWAYS

Granny's canary
Escaped from its cage
It's up on the roof
In a terrible rage

Hurling abuse
And making demands
That granny fails
To understand

'Lack of privacy'
'Boring old food'
It holds up placards
Painted and rude

It's not coming down
The canary warns
Till gran carries out
Major reforms.

The message has spread
And now for days
Cage-birds have been acting
In very strange ways.

MRS MOON

Mrs Moon
sitting up in the sky
little old lady
rock–a–bye
with a ball of fading light
and silvery needles
knitting the night

HAIKU

Snowman in a field
listening to the raindrops
wishing him farewell

GRUESOME

I was sitting in the sitting room
toying with some toys
when from a door marked: 'GRUESOME'
there came a GRUESOME noise

Cautiously I opened it
and there to my surprise
a little GRUE sat sitting
with tears in its eyes

'Oh little GRUE please tell me
what is it ails thee so?'
'Well I'm so small,' he sobbed,
'GRUESSES don't want to know'

'Exercises are the answer,
each morning you must DO SOME'
He thanked me, smiled,
and do you know what?
The very next day he . . .

THE SOUND COLLECTOR

A stranger called this morning
Dressed all in black and grey
Put every sound into a bag
And carried them away

The whistling of the kettle
The turning of the lock
The purring of the kitten
The ticking of the clock

The popping of the toaster
The crunching of the flakes
When you spread the marmalade
The scraping noise it makes

The hissing of the frying-pan
The ticking of the grill
The bubbling of the bathtub
As it starts to fill

The drumming of the raindrops
On the window-pane
When you do the washing-up
The gurgle of the drain

The crying of the baby
The squeaking of the chair
The swishing of the curtain
The creaking of the stair

A stranger called this morning
He didn't leave his name
Left us only silence
Life will never be the same.

THE READER OF THIS POEM

The reader of this poem
Is as cracked as a cup
As daft as treacle-toffee
As mucky as a pup

As troublesome as bubblegum
As brash as a brush
As bouncy as a double-tum
As quiet as a sshhh . . .

As sneaky as a witch's spell
As tappytoe as jazz
As empty as a wishing-well
As echoey as as as as as as . . .

As bossy as a whistle
As prickly as a pair
Of boots made out of thistles
And elephant hair

As vain as trainers
As boring as a draw
As smelly as a drain is
Outside the kitchen door

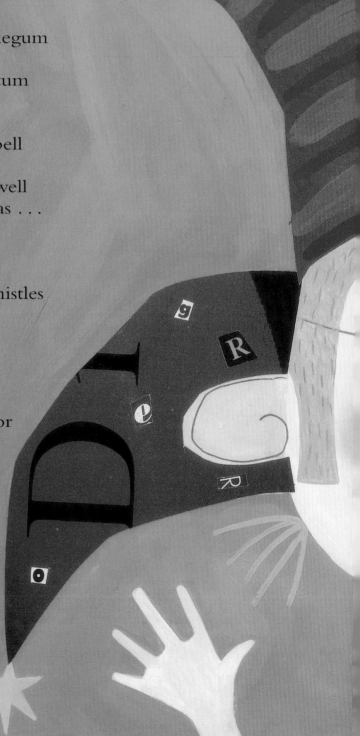

As hungry as a wave
That feeds upon the coast
As gaping as the grave
As GOTCHA! as a ghost

As fruitless as a cake of soap
As creeping-up as smoke
The reader of this poem, I hope,
Knows how to take a joke!

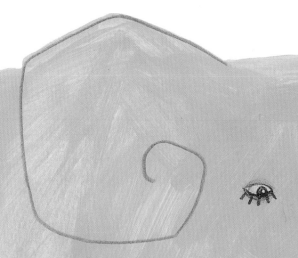

ELEPHANT

If I could be reincarnated
    (And who knows, I might have been already?)
Then I'd like to return as an elephant
    Reliable and steady.

Big as a room filled with sunshine
    A giant, gentle and strong,
Lord of the manor
    I'd roam the savannah
Trumpeting all day long.

At sunset it's down to the river
    To meet my old pals for a chat
After a few bouts of trunk-wrestling
    We'd squirt water, do daft things like that.

Then tired and happy we'd lumber home
    Humming an elephant tune
Thinking our thanks to our maker
    By the light of an elephant moon.

If I could be reincarnated
    An elephant I would choose.
Failing that Napoleon,
    Kim Basinger or Ted Hughes.

Love a Duck

I love a duck called Jack
He's my very favourite pet
But last week he took poorly
So I took him to the vet.

The vet said: 'Lad, the news is bad,
Your duck has lost its quack
And there's nowt veterinary science
Can do to bring it back.'

A quackless duck? What thankless luck!
Struck dumb without a word
Rendered mute like a bunged-up flute
My splendid, tongue-tied bird.

All day now on the duvet
He sits and occasionally sighs
Dreaming up a miracle
A faraway look in his eyes.

Like an orphan for his mother
Like a maiden for her lover
Waiting silently is Jack
For the gab to come back

For the gift of tongues that goes . . .

Benjamin Zephaniah Interviewed by Brian Patten

You've got a fantastic name – Benjamin Obadiah Iqbal Zephaniah – do the separate names have a special meaning?

Benjamin means 'son of the right hand of God', and as a Rastafarian it is also the name of my tribe. Obadiah means 'messenger of God', which is a good job description. Iqbal is an Islamic word meaning 'success, good fortune and luck'! Zephaniah means 'God has preserved'.

You believe in God?

Yes, but I can see the good and bad in all religions and I never preach in my work.

How about school? You were a bit rebellious.

I didn't do well at school and I think the main reason was it was all reading, writing and arithmetic – there was no poetry, no music. I felt I was being prepared for a life as a mechanic or plumber or even a sports person, which are all fine, but I wanted to be an intellectual. I knew what I wanted to do for my school, but my school did not know what to do for me.

My schooldays were a bit the same. I got caned once for stepping out of line. I was just kicking some broken glass into the gutter in case a cat or a dog stepped on it, and when I explained this to the teacher he was furious with me for answering back.

I was one of those kids that kept asking *Why?* Once I received some of the answers, I realized that those in authority were not right, so I could not go along with them.

Have you a favourite line by another poet?

'Most people ignore most poetry because most poetry ignores most people.' It was said by Adrian Mitchell. I know it may not be called a poem, but I think it's so true and something I want to see change.

You were born in England but you've visited Jamaica a lot. How old were you when you went for the first time?

I was nine. It was very different to England. I could hardly find anything the same. In Jamaica, music could be heard all day, there were outdoor schools and lots of animals.

You seem very fond of animals. You had a cat called Danny once, which you've written about. Have you a favourite animal?

I love lions, but I think all animals are equal.

I wish my cat, Wiz, did. He's always chasing other cats out of the garden.

I let half the garden of my last home in London go completely wild, and this attracted hedgehogs, foxes and frogs into it. I had the company of a monkey for two weeks once and it was great fun. But you need a lot of energy to keep up with them. They can get up to very naughty things!

TALKING TURKEYS!!

Be nice to yu turkeys dis christmas
  Cos turkeys jus wanna hav fun
  Turkeys are cool, turkeys are wicked
  An every turkey has a Mum.
  Be nice to yu turkeys dis christmas,
  Don't eat it, keep it alive,
  It could be yu mate an not on yu plate
Say, Yo! Turkey I'm on your side.

I got lots of friends who are turkeys
An all of dem fear christmas time,
Dey wanna enjoy it, dey say humans destroyed it
An humans are out of dere mind,
Yeah, I got lots of friends who are turkeys
Dey all hav a right to a life,
Not to be caged up an genetically made up
By any farmer an his wife.

Turkeys jus wanna play reggae
Turkeys jus wanna hip-hop
Can yu imagine a nice young turkey saying,
'I cannot wait for de chop'?
Turkeys like getting presents, dey wanna watch
  christmas TV,
Turkeys hav brains an turkeys feel pain
In many ways like yu an me.

I once knew a turkey called
Turkey
He said, 'Benji explain to me please,
Who put de turkey in christmas
An what happens to christmas trees?'
I said, 'I am not too sure turkey
But it's nothing to do wid Christ Mass
Humans get greedy an waste more dan need be
An business men mek loadsa cash.'

Be nice to yu turkey dis christmas
Invite dem indoors fe sum greens
Let dem eat cake an let dem partake
In a plate of organic grown beans,
Be nice to yu turkey dis christmas
An spare dem de cut of de knife,
Join Turkeys United an dey'll be delighted
An yu will mek new friends '**FOR LIFE**'.

LUV SONG

I am in luv wid a hedgehog
I've never felt dis way before
I have luv fe dis hedgehog
An everyday I luv her more an more,
She lives by de shed
Where weeds an roses bed
An I just want de world to know
She makes me glow.

I am in luv wid a hedgehog
She's making me hair stand on edge,
So in luv wid dis hedgehog
An her friends
Who all live in de hedge
She visits me late
An eats off Danny's plate
But Danny's a cool tabby cat
He leaves it at dat.

I am in luv wid a hedgehog,
She's gone away so I must wait
But I do miss my hedgehog
Everytime she goes to hibernate.

FAIR PLAY

Mirror mirror on the wall
Could you please return our ball
Our football went through your crack
You have two now
Give one back.

CIVIL LIES

Dear Teacher,

When I was born in Ethiopia
Life began.
As I sailed down the Nile civilization began.
When I stopped to think universities were built.
When I set sail
Asians and true Americans sailed with me.

When we traded nations were built.
We did not have animals.
Animals lived with us.
We had so much time
Thirteen months made our year.
We created social services
And cities that still stand.

So teacher do not say
Colombus discovered me
Check the great things I was doing
Before I suffered slavery.

Yours truly,

Mr Africa

NATURAL ANTHEM

God save our gracious green
Long live our glorious scene
God save our green.

Dis ting is serious
Do it for all of us
Save our asparagus,
God save
Our
Green.

SOLIDARITY

An army of militant greens
In bio-degradable genes
Shout 'Give peas a chance
An lettuce all dance
In unity wid butter beans'.

BODY TALK

Dere's a Sonnet
Under me bonnet
Dere's a Epic
In me ear,
Dere's a Novel
In me navel
Dere's a Classic
Here somewhere.
Dere's a Movie
In me left knee
A long story
In me right,
Dere's a shorty
Inbetweeny
It is tickly
In de night.
Dere's a picture
In me ticker
Unmixed riddims
In me heart,
In me texture
Dere's a comma
In me fat chin
Dere is Art.

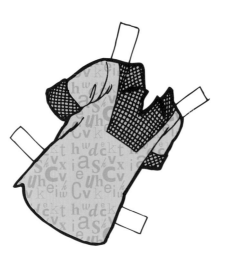

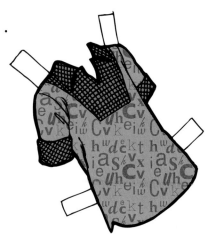

Dere's an Opera
In me bladder
A Ballad's
In me wrist
Dere is laughter
In me shoulder
In me guzzard's
A nice twist.
In me dreadlocks
Dere is syntax
A dance kicks
In me bum
Thru me blood tracks
Dere run true facts
I got limericks
From me Mum,
Documentaries
In me entries
Plays on history
In me folk,
Dere's a Trilogy
When I tink of three
On me toey
Dere's a joke.

FOR WORD

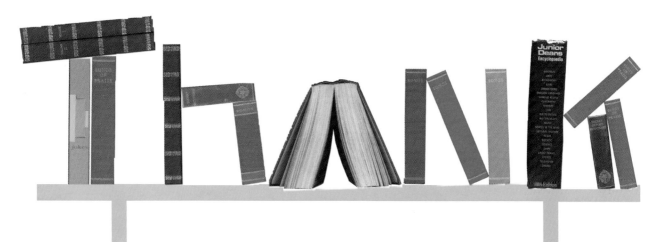

◆ **Thank you** for the *words* I read
Thank you for the **words** I need
Thank you for the WORDS so great
Thanks for 𝔴𝔬𝔯𝔡𝔰 that raise debate,
Thanks for the **words** on my bookshelf
Thanx for the **words** I make myself
Thank you for **words** that make me cry
And words that leave me feeling dry.

❝ **Thanks** for WORDS that do inspire
And those *words* that burn like fire
Thanks for all the *words* I note
Thank you for all the *words* I quote,
I thank you for the **words** like me
Thanks for 𝒲𝒪𝑅𝒟𝒮 that set me free
And I thank you for *words* like you
I always need a word or two.

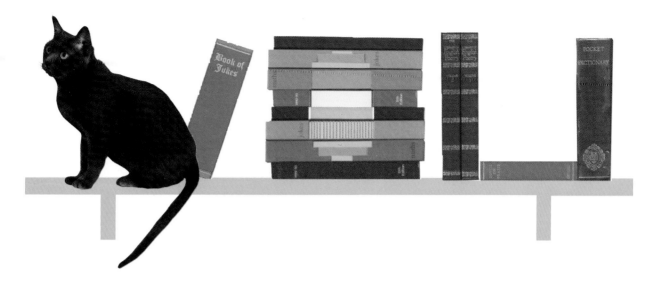

Thanks for **words** that make things plain
And words that help me to explain
Thanks for **words** that make life fun
And *words* that help me overcome,
Thanks for **words** that make me rap
Thanks for *words* that make me clap
Thanks for WORDS that make me smile
Thanks for WORDS with grace and style.

Thanks for all those **words** that sing
Thanks for **words** are everything
Thanks for all the **WORDS** like this
And little sloppy *words* like kiss,
Thanks for **words** like hip-hooray
And those cool **words** I like to say
Thanks for *words* that reach and touch
Thank you very, very much.

WALKING BLACK HOME

That day waz
A bad day,

I walked for
Many miles,

Unlike me,
I did not

Return any
Smiles.

Tired,

Weak
And
Hungry,

But I
Would not
Turn

Back,

Sometimes it's hard
To get a taxi
When you're **Black.**

THIS ORANGE TREE

✾ **I** touched my first rose
Under this orange tree,
I was young and fruity
The sweet rose was blooming.

✝ **I** found faith
Under this orange tree
It was here all the time.
One day I picked it up
Then I realized
How great you are.

👓 **It** was under this
Very orange tree
That I read
My first Martin Luther King speech.
How great the word.

♪ **It** was here
Under this very orange tree,
On this very peace of earth
That I first sang
With a hummingbird.
How great the song.

❤ **This** orange tree knows me,
It is my friend,
I trust it and
It taste good.

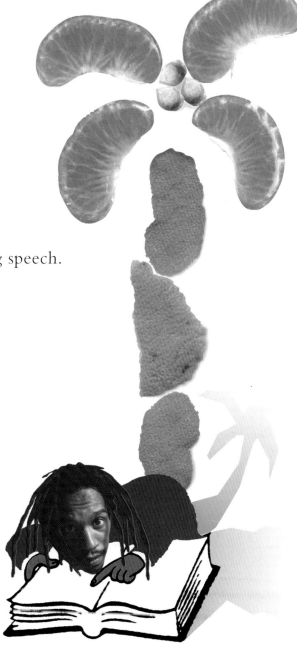

BRIAN PATTEN INTERVIEWED BY WIZ

Did you start writing so you'd have enough money to buy me fish?

Of course not. I was about thirteen when I began writing. It was a way of expressing feelings I felt I couldn't share with the adults who surrounded me.

Thirteen! That's about ninety-one in cat years.

Well, I'm not a cat. Now stop interrupting me, Wiz. Let me –

Where do you get your ideas from?

They're all over the place. Sometimes I think if ideas were visible, the world would be so cluttered there wouldn't be room to swing a cat.

I should hope not!

Sometimes ideas are sparked off by a rhyme, but I honestly don't know where they come from. All I know is that as soon as I get one another comes along, then another, then another. And then they go away for a while, and I think I'll never be able to write another poem ever again.

I'm glad you're a writer, because you can stay home all day and feed me. But do you actually enjoy writing?

Yes, especially when you aren't climbing all over my desk. Sometimes I find it hard to sit down and begin new work. For me, writing comes in bursts of activity with long stretches of nothing in between. When I'm not writing I forget how much I like it when I am.

Of all the poems you've written, which is your favourite?

If I told you that then all the other poems would get jealous.

Well, I think your best poems are about cats. I don't suppose you can remember your childhood – after all, it was about 280 cat years ago – but if you can, can you recall any special cat who got you interested in books?

I'm afraid not, but there was a lady I called Aunt Lizzy, who wasn't really my aunt. She used to buy me books. And before that there was a woman called Frieda, who lived alone in a little house down our street. Her living room was full of dust and mothball-scented books. She gave me a book of fairytales, and *The Little Mermaid* (who leaves the ocean to be with the man she loves) was one of the stories in the book. When the mermaid leaves the ocean she feels as if she is walking on broken glass. The beauty and the cruelty of that story really impressed me.

Have you any advice for people who want to write?

Yes. Keep the cat off your desk.

THE RACE TO GET TO SLEEP

They're on their marks, they're set,
They're off!

Matthew's kicking off his shoes!
Penny's struggling out of her jumper!
He's ripping off his trousers!
She's got one sock off! Now the other's off!
But Matthew's still winning! No, he's not!
It's Penny! Penny's in the lead!
She's down to her knickers!
She's racing out of the room!
She's racing upstairs!
Matthew's right behind her!
There's a fight on the landing!
There's a scramble at the bathroom door!
It's Penny! It's Matthew! It's . . .
Splash! They're both in the bath!
But there's a hitch!
Matthew's got soap in his eye!
Penny's got soap up her nose!
They're stalling! But no, they're both fine!
They're both out the bath! They're neck and neck!
It's Matthew! It's Penny! It's Matthew!
Now it's Penny again! She's ahead!
She's first on with her pyjamas!
Now Matthew's catching up! There's nothing in it!
They're climbing into their beds!
Matthew's in the lead with one eye closed!
Now it's Penny again! She's got both closed!
So's Matthew! He's catching up!
It's impossible to tell who's winning!
They're both absolutely quiet!

There's not a murmur from either of them.
It's Matthew! It's Penny! It's . . .
It's a draw! A draw!
But no! Wait a moment! It's not a draw!
Matthew's opened an eye!
He's asking if Penny's asleep yet!
He's disqualified!
So's Penny! She's doing the same!
She's asking if Matthew's asleep yet!
It's impossible! It's daft!
It's the hardest race in the world!

DON'T FORGET TO WASH BEHIND YOUR HEARING-AID!

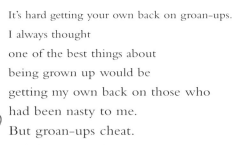

It's hard getting your own back on groan-ups.
I always thought
one of the best things about
being grown up would be
getting my own back on those who
had been nasty to me.
But groan-ups cheat.
While you are busy growing up
they think: 'Hu, hu, there's that boy
I was nasty to, and he's nearly
old enough to get his own back!'
They feel they're under attack
and start to shrink. I think
they do it on purpose. They get
all frail and wizeny-looking
and you just can't go around
getting your own back on little old ladies
and wrinkly little men
who were nasty when
you were ten.
You can't twist their ears
or shake them by the shoulder
and shout, 'Take your teeth out!
Brush them immediately!
You'd better obey me!'
or
'Don't forget to wash behind your hearing-aid!'
The trouble is you don't even want to.
Groan-ups always win.
It's one of the hard, hard facts of life.

HIDE-AWAY SAM

Hide-away Sam sat in the darkness,
Pale as the day he was born,
A miser who stored up his blessings
Yet looked on blessings with scorn.

He peeked through a chink in the doorway,
A crack on which the sun shone
All the things he had craved danced past him,
He blinked, and they were gone.

A ladder was stretched up to Heaven,
Its rungs were covered in dew,
At its foot was a bucket of diamonds
(From the sky God had stolen a few)

And beyond the ladder an orchard
Where bees dunked in pollen flew
Between the falling blossom
And the core of a fruit that was new.

'Time to come out and enjoy life!'
A voice boomed down from above.
'Time to swap ten aeons of darkness
For one bright second of love.'

But Hide-away Sam shrank inwards.
He refused to open the door.
The Angel of Mercy lost patience,
Shrugged, and said no more.

MUM WON'T LET ME KEEP A RABBIT

Mum won't let me keep a rabbit,
She won't let me keep a bat,
She won't let me keep a porcupine
Or a water-rat.

I can't keep pigeons
And I can't keep snails,
I can't keep kangaroos
Or wallabies with nails.

She won't let me keep a rattle-snake
Or viper in the house,
She won't let me keep a mamba
Or its meal, a mouse.

She won't let me keep a wombat
And it isn't very clear
Why I can't keep iguanas,
Jelly-fish or deer.

I can't keep a cockroach
Or a bumble-bee,
I can't keep an earwig,
A maggot or a flea.

I can't keep a wildebeest
And it's just my luck
I can't keep a mallard,
A dabchick or a duck.

She won't let me keep piranhas,
Toads or even frogs,
She won't let me keep an octopus
Or muddy water-hogs.

So out in the garden I keep a pet ant
And up in the attic
A SECRET ELEPHANT!

RABBIT'S SPRING

Snow
goes,

Ice
thaws,

Warm
paws!

SQUEEZES

We love to squeeze bananas,
We love to squeeze ripe plums,
And when they are feeling sad
We love to squeeze our mums.

UNCLE BEN FROM NUMBER ONE

Uncle Ben was not a hen
But when he laid an egg
He did it quite professionally
By lifting up a leg.

He studied it and prodded it
And said, 'I'm mystified.'
And then he took it
to the kitchen
Where he had it, fried.

LOOKING FOR DAD

Whenever Mum and Dad
were full of gloom
they always yelled,
'TIDY UP YOUR ROOM!'
Just because my comics were
scattered here and
everywhere and
because I did not care
where I left my underwear
they yelled, 'YOU CAN'T WATCH TV TODAY
IF YOU DON'T TIDY ALL THOSE THINGS AWAY!'
Then one day they
could not care less
about the room's
awful mess.
They seemed more intent
on having a domestic argument.
They both looked glum
and instead of me Dad
screeched at Mum.
One night when I
went to bed he
simply vanished.
I had not tidied
up my room because
I too was
full of gloom.
That night I dreamt
Dad was hidden
beneath the things
I'd been given.
In my dream
I was in despair

and flung about
my underwear
but could not find
him anywhere.
I looked for Dad
lots and lots
beneath crumpled sheets
and old robots.
I looked in cupboards
and in shoes,
I looked up all
the chimney flues.
I remembered how
he'd seemed to be
unhappier than
even me. When I woke I knew
it was not my room
that filled Mum and Dad
with so much gloom.
Now I stare at all
my old toy cars
and carpets stained
with old Mars bars
and hope he will
come back soon
and admire my very tidy room.

THE TREE AND THE POOL

'I don't want my leaves to drop,' said the tree.
'I don't want to freeze,' said the pool.
'I don't want to smile,' said the sombre man,
'Or ever to cry,' said the Fool.

'I don't want to open,' said the bud,
'I don't want to end,' said the night.
'I don't want to rise,' said the neap-tide,
'Or ever to fall,' said the kite.

They wished and they murmured and whispered,
They said that to change was a crime,
Then a voice from nowhere answered,
'You must do what I say,' said Time.

THE WHALE'S HYMN

In an ocean before cold dawn broke

Covered by an overcoat

I lay awake in a boat

And heard a whale.

Hearing a song so solemn and so calm

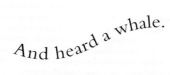

It seemed absurd to feel alarm –

For I had a notion it sang

God's favourite hymn,

And spoke direct to Him.

JACKIE KAY INTERVIEWED BY BRIAN PATTEN

You were very young when you had your first poem published. Was it exciting?

Yes, it was very exciting. I was twelve, and the poem was about poverty in Glasgow tenements. I can still remember it. It was called 'Hard Times'. It was very sentimental.

Do you know why you started writing?

I liked making things up – lies, stories, poems, rhymes. I used to make up a lot of lies, and writing allowed me to tell lies without getting into trouble. I liked reading them to friends in the school lunch hour. I also discovered that writing could keep me company when I felt isolated.

You must have had a fantastic imagination when you were little. Did you ever make up any imaginary friends?

I had an imaginary friend who existed for two whole years. My family believed he was real. He was called Brendon Gallacher. I wrote a poem about him. He was a lot nicer than some of my real friends. I loved him. But when my parents found out he didn't exist, that killed him. He had to die! Even now, the word for lie in my family is Brendon Gallacher.

Did I ever tell you that my cat, Wiz, used to belong to a famous wizard and knows how to cast spells on dogs and turn them into yoghurt?

That's a great big Brendon Gallacher, Brian!

You've written about being bullied and hurt by racist remarks. How old were you when you were first aware of racism?

I think I first became aware of racism when I went to school. Other kids at school would call me names or tell racist jokes or follow me, and I found all this upsetting and humiliating. But I made it my business to fight back. I had no black teachers in my primary school and apart from my brother there were no other black kids in the school.

When you were growing up in Glasgow, what kinds of things did you spend your pocket money on?

I spent it on Enid Blyton books or packets of elastic bands to play what we called Chinese ropes, or on pokey hats – that was our word for ice-cream cones. I liked buying lots of sharp pencils and rubbers. Sometimes, to annoy my brother, I saved my pocket money and put it in my bank book so that in a few weeks' time I could buy something big. How about you? You are asking us poets lots of questions. What did you spend your pocket money on?

Oh, I never spent one penny of it. I saved every single penny of my pocket money throughout my entire childhood so that when I grew up I could buy a fabulous cat from a great wizard.

That's another Brendon Gallacher, Brian!

PUMPKIN FOR MAXINE

On Hallowe'en Mum and I made a pumpkin lantern;
huge triangular eyes and a square nose.
It cried when we dug out its pyramid teeth:
Ouch, it said, *this is worse than the dentist.*
I got a fright; but the strangest thing was,
my mum didn't hear it. *Dentists at least give gas,*
Pumpkin complained. There was my mum, oblivious,
still hacking out its brain. 'Come on. Dig in,' she says,
'this is taking hours; it'll turn back into a carriage.'
I started feeling dizzy, giddy, all out of sorts.
I tried to hold its jaw closed so it couldn't talk.
Ouch, it said, *my cheekbone; do I have to be hollow?*
'Of course you do,' I whispered, 'this is all hallow's
eve. We will put a candle in the hollow.' *Oh no,*
screamed Pumpkin. *I'm going to burn, my skull.*
Worse than Catherine. Suddenly, Pumpkin rolled
off the table. 'Look what you've done!' shouted Mum.
'You careless thing.' 'It wasn't me,' I said breathless,
and pleased. Pumpkin was trying to escape.
'Oh, for goodness' sake,' said Mum.
'What's the matter with your head?'
It's not her head, Pumpkin said, *It's mine.*
I've got a dreadful headache, got anything for it?
But, my mum, who'd suddenly, finally heard it —
Pumpkin's piercing voice — fainted, falling
into the basin with all the apples for the dooking.

I'M NOT OLD ENOUGH YET

Even at three, this business of a big man
coming down the chimney loaded with pressies
from your list (who showed it to him?
Why wasn't he covered in soot?) seemed a bit far-fetched.
Especially since we didn't have a chimney.
But later I started to believe in this man
with the beard longer than God's.
I left food out. I tried to stay awake.
I still suspected Santa was a black woman dressed in red,
but I never, since three, asked my mum any questions.
Now I'm seven. A pal of mine asks, 'Do you believe
in Santa Claus?' *What do you mean?* 'Do you think it's true,'
she continued until my mouth fell open and I started to scream:
You shouldn't have told me. I'm not old enough yet.

NEW BABY

My baby brother makes so much noise
that the Rottweiler next door
phoned up to complain.

My baby brother makes so much noise
that all the big green frogs
came out the drains.

My baby brother makes so much noise
that the rats and the mice
wore headphones.

My baby brother makes so much noise
that I can't ask my mum a question,
so much noise that sometimes

I think of sitting the cat on top of him
in his pretty little cot with all his teddies.
But even the cat is terrified of his cries.

So I have devised a plan. A soundproof room.
A telephone to talk to my mum.
A small lift to receive food and toys.

Thing is, it will cost a fortune.
The other thing is, the frogs have gone.
It's not bad now. Not that I like him or anything.

BRENDON GALLACHER (FOR MY BROTHER MAXIE)

He was seven and I was six, my Brendon Gallacher.
He was Irish and I was Scottish, my Brendon Gallacher.
His father was in prison; he was a cat burglar.
My father was a communist party full-time worker.
He had six brothers and I had one, my Brendon Gallacher.

He would hold my hand and take me by the river
Where we'd talk all about his family being poor.
He'd get his mum out of Glasgow when he got older.
A wee holiday some place nice. Some place far.
I'd tell my mum about my Brendon Gallacher

How his mum drank and his daddy was a cat burglar.
And she'd say, 'Why not have him round to dinner?'
No, no, I'd say, he's got big holes in his trousers.
I like meeting him by the burn in the open air.
Then one day after we'd been friends two years,

One day when it was pouring and I was indoors,
My mum says to me, 'I was talking to Mrs Moir
Who lives next door to your Brendon Gallacher
Didn't you say his address was 24 Novar?
She says there are no Gallachers at 24 Novar

There never have been any Gallachers next door.'
And he died then, my Brendon Gallacher,
Flat out on my bedroom floor, his spiky hair,
His impish grin, his funny flapping ear.
Oh Brendon. Oh my Brendon Gallacher.

THE WANT-WANT TWINS

We are the Want-Want Twins.
We go from shop to shop.
We are the Want-Want Twins.
We don't know how to stop.
One day it's a bow and arrow.
Another it's a dinosaur.
What are we going to get tomorrow?
More. More. More.

We are the Want-Want Twins.
Our eyes sharp shiny pins.
Our hands quick shark's fins.
We go from shop to shop.
One day it's the game Frustration.
We don't know what we need.
Another it is compensation.
Greed. Greed. Greed.

We are the Want-Want Twins.
We're completely over the top.
We are the Want-Want Twins.
We don't know how to stop.
We send our parents every night
A list that goes like this:
2 new bikes. Don't be tight.
X.X.X.

We are the Want–Want Twins.
Money grows on trees.
We are the Want–Want Twins.
We are the bee's knees.
All we want is everything.
We don't know how to stop.
We will be the Want–Want Twins till we

drop

drop

drop.

THE SCHOOL HAMSTER'S HOLIDAY

Remember the coal bunker in winter?
Naw? You wouldn't want to, either.
Stooping at the grate gathering auld ash.

Always leaving a wee bed of ash
for the next fire's blazing dreams.
Heeking a' that heavy coal from the bunker.

The big black jewels in the steel bucket.
Toast from the naked flame was a treat,
or burning pink and white marshmallows

till they caved in and surrendered.
But that was rare.
This is what I most remember:

The time when Snowie, our school hamster,
came home for a weekend holiday with me.
A cage is a cage no matter where the house is,

thinks Snowie, probably, so come night-time
she escapes her prison, come night-time
she fancies a night in a Slumberdown,

climbs up the chimney breast
into the ma and da's bed.
You should have heard them scream

when they woke to see Snowie,
now the colour of soot, no snaw,
running the course of the duvet.

They were big screams like this:
AAAAAAAAAAAAAAAAAAAAAAAAAAAAAA
AAAAAAAAAAAAAAAAAAAAHHHHHHHHHH

I spent the rest of the weekend
tight-lipped and desperate,
sponging that hamster with all my might

my wee yellow sponge going like a wiper,
hearing children chant in my ears,
She's made our Snowie into a darkie.

I tried and tried to make Snowie white.
It wis an impossible task.
Have you ever tried to shammy a hammy?

Monday morning was an absolute disgrace.
I'll never forget the shame of it.
The wee GREY hamster looking po-faced.

115

WAVES

There are waves to chase and waves that crash,
There are waves to jump like skipping ropes,
Waves to run away to sand, waves to leap and bound.
Waves that are turquoise, waves that are brown,
Waves full of seaweed, waves that drown.
Waves clear and calm, waves angry and wronged,
Waves that whisper, waves that roar like thunder,
Waves you'd never swim under, pounding rocks and shore.
Waves that put you to sleep, sssh sssh sssh cradle-rock.
Waves that look like sea horses or sheep or curly froth.
Waves that are cold as bare floor, waves that are warm as toast.
There are waves called the Black Sea, the Red Sea, the North Sea,
Waves called the Pacific Ocean, the Atlantic Ocean, the Antarctic.
If you counted them all, wave upon wave upon wave
Would it be a hundred, a thousand, a billion – or more?

NAMES

Today my best pal, *my number one*,
called me a *dirty darkie*,
when I wouldn't give her a sweetie.
I said, softly, 'I would never believe
you of all people, Char Hardy,
would say that word to me.
Others, yes, the ones
that are stupid and ignorant,
and don't know better, but
not you, Char Hardy, not you.
I thought I could trust you.
I thought you were different.
But I must have been mistaken.'

Char went a very strange colour.
Said a most peculiar, 'Sorry,'
as if she was swallowing her voice.
Grabbed me, hugged me, begged me
to forgive her. She was crying.
I didn't mean it. I didn't mean it.
I felt the playground sink. *Sorry. Sorry.*
A see-saw rocked, crazy, all by itself.
An orange swing swung high on its own.
My voice was hard as a steel frame:
'Well then, what exactly did you mean?'

John Agard Interviewed by Brian Patten

Tell me a bit about your childhood.

I was born and grew up in Guyana with my mother, who towed me religiously at the back of her bike to a Roman Catholic primary school. My mother and father are both Guyanese and I'm a town boy, as they say, for I was born in Georgetown. It was once known as the garden city of the Caribbean. There were lots of avenues lined with flamboyant trees.

Was there a special place in the city you remember?

As a child I loved going to the Botanical Gardens. That's where the zoo and my favourite spot in it were – the manatee pond.

Manatees are . . . ?

Sea cows. All you had to do was whistle, and after a while the manatees would swim up to the top and push out their big mouths for handfuls of grass. They say the manatees gave rise to the mermaid legend.

You were nearly thirty when you left the Caribbean for Britain. Were you sad to leave?

I was both sad and excited. Sad to leave my mother, of course, and friends, the people I'd grown up with. But I was excited at the thought of coming to the UK, where my father had already settled, and where it was possible to consider becoming a full-time writer. I was also excited by the possibility of seeing snow. I used to think snow fell in big lumps. I didn't realize it fell in those fleeting flakes. That's why in one poem I've written I speak of snowflakes as tiny insects drifting down.

Did you always want to be a poet?

At one time I played with the idea of becoming a priest, maybe because most of my secondary school teachers were priests, and when I was about twelve I used to serve as an altar boy. At home I even pretended to be a priest, dragging a long sheet over my shoulders and chanting away in Latin, while my cousin would be kneeling before me and pouring out a little wine we had pinched from an uncle. I also wanted to be an actor, a lawyer and, of course, a cricket commentator!

Do you write lots of drafts of your poems?

I like playing with a poem inside of me so that, by the time I get to the page, the poem is well on the way. But on the page there's still chipping and pruning to be done. Even if a poem happens to come fairly quickly, there may be one bit of tightening up needed to make it work, but it can take months, even years, before you come to recognize that small change staring you in the face.

I know you like music. You've lots of instruments in your house – an old piano, a marimba, flutes and small percussion instruments. Does music always influence your poems?

Even though I don't play any of these instruments very well, I like having them around, like ancestral presences, and playing around when I'm in the mood. And even if it isn't conscious – in the sense of exploring, say, the rhythm of calypso or blues, or a spell or chant – I'd say a poem is ever seeking to sing its way into our memory.

Oh, before I forget, Wiz told me to send his best wishes to your cat, Corvetta. He says one day he hopes to get together with all the other poets' cats and hold a great big poetry reading. I'm not sure I like the idea very much though – can you imagine a huge gang of cats sitting around wailing?

You never know, the poems might sound great in cat language.

John Agard

SPELL TO BRING A SMILE

Come down Rainbow
Rainbow come down

I have a space for you
in my small face

If my face is too small for you
take a space in my chest

If my chest is too small for you
take a space in my belly

If my belly is too small for you
then take every part of me

Come down Rainbow
Rainbow come down

You can eat me from head to toe

THE CLOWN'S LAST JOKE

Whatever became of the clown's red nose?

They found a farewell note
in a bundle of tricks

They found a shaggy eyebrow
under a floppy hat

They found a painted cheek
inside a grinning shoe

They found a rubber ball
between baggy trousers

But they never found the clown's red nose

They pulled out drawers
They turned over sheets

But whatever became of the clown's red nose
only God in heaven knows

HATCH ME A RIDDLE

In a little white room
all round and smooth
sits a yellow moon.

In a little white room
once open, for ever open,
sits a yellow moon.

In a little white room,
with neither window nor door,
sits a yellow moon.

Who will break the walls
of the little white room
to steal the yellow moon?
A wise one or a fool?

THE HURT BOY AND THE BIRDS

The hurt boy talked to the birds
and fed them the crumbs of his heart.

It was not easy to find the words
for secrets he hid under his skin.
The hurt boy spoke of a bully's fist
that made his face a bruised moon —
his spectacles stamped to ruin.

It was not easy to find the words
for things that nightly hissed
as if his pillow was a hideaway for creepy-crawlies —
the note sent to the girl he fancied
held high in mockery.

But the hurt boy talked to the birds
and their feathers gave him welcome —

Their wings taught him new ways to become.

ONCE UPON A TIME

Once upon a time there lived
a small joke
in the middle of nowhere.

This small joke
was dying to share
itself with someone

but nobody came to hear
this small joke.

So this small joke told
itself to the birds

and the birds told this small joke to the trees
and the trees told this small joke to the rivers
and the rivers told this small joke to the mountains
and the mountains told this small joke to the stars

till the whole world
started to swell with laughter

and nobody believed
it all began
with a small joke

that lived in the middle of nowhere.

Everybody kept saying

it was me
it was me.

A Date with Spring

Got a date with Spring
 Got to look me best.
 Of all the trees
   I'll be the smartest dressed.

   Perfumed breeze
   behind me ear.
   Pollen accessories
   all in place.
   Raindrop moisturizer
   for me face.
   Sunlight tints
   to spruce up the hair.

   What's the good of being a tree
 if you can't flaunt your beauty?

Winter, I was naked.
 Exposed as can be.
 Me wardrobe took off
   with the wind.
   Life was a frosty slumber.
    Now, Spring, here I come.
    Can't wait to slip in
     to me little green number.

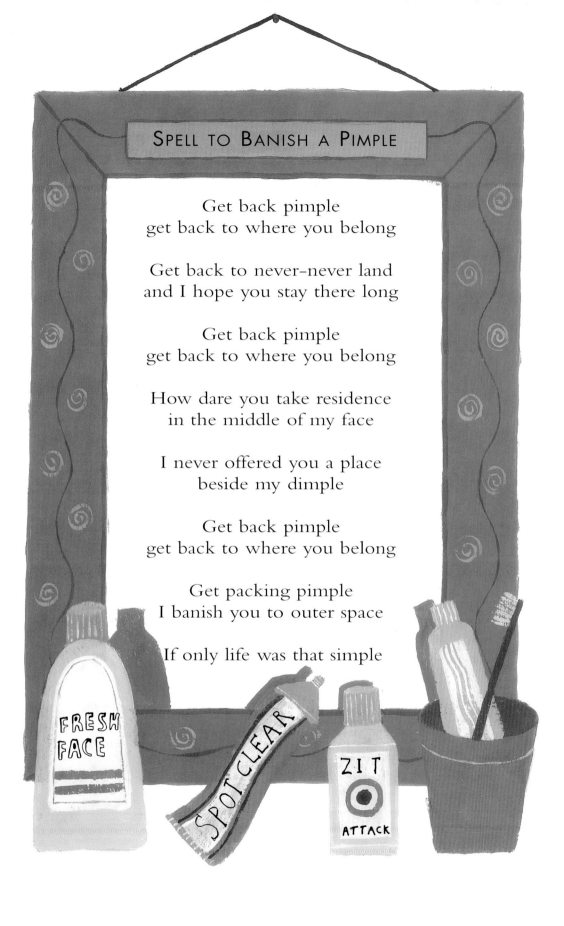

SPELL TO BANISH A PIMPLE

Get back pimple
get back to where you belong

Get back to never-never land
and I hope you stay there long

Get back pimple
get back to where you belong

How dare you take residence
in the middle of my face

I never offered you a place
beside my dimple

Get back pimple
get back to where you belong

Get packing pimple
I banish you to outer space

If only life was that simple

FRESH FACE

SPOTCLEAR

ZIT
ATTACK

FISHERMAN CHANT

Sister river
Brother river
Mother river
Father river
O life giver
O life taker
O friend river
What have you
in store
for a poor
fisherman
today?

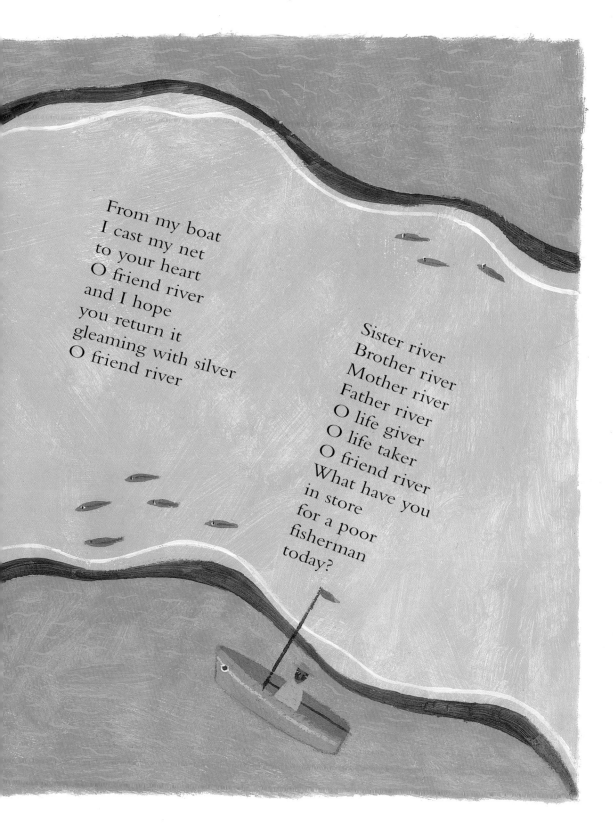

From my boat
I cast my net
to your heart
O friend river
and I hope
you return it
gleaming with silver
O friend river

Sister river
Brother river
Mother river
Father river
O life giver
O life taker
O friend river
What have you
in store
for a poor
fisherman
today?

Allan Ahlberg Interviewed by Brian Patten

Is there a poem by someone else you wish you'd written?

Yes, two actually: 'Elegy Written in a Country Churchyard' (Thomas Gray) and 'Humpty Dumpty' (anon.).

I always used to think the word 'anon.' was the name of an old poet until my teacher explained it meant someone unknown. Did you have a favourite teacher?

Not so much a favourite teacher, but in a way the one who affected me the most was Miss Scriven. She got me writing. Miss Scriven gave marks for handwriting, and mine was dreadful, and punctuation, which I placed little trust in. Also I often wrote in a state of high excitement and left words out. The important thing about Miss Scriven was when she returned our work she would encourage us to read it aloud to the rest of the class. When it was my turn I discovered that, read aloud, the story would come alive. I could *read* my own handwriting – more or less – and the absence of punctuation didn't matter and the missing words I could put back in. And the other children – the stories I wrote set out to be funny – laughed.

I bet that felt great. I think if school-friends like what you do, it encourages you as much as anything. Before you became a professional writer you had lots of jobs – including being a gravedigger. Was that a scary job?

Not really. I got the better part of my education in that cemetery. In winter I would dig hard and fast like an armadillo, get down out of the wind, pull a paperback out of my pocket, lean against my little ladder – and read. In summer I would shuffle with my scythe – really! –

between the gravestones, rake the cut grass into a convenient pile, slump down behind it like Little Boy Blue – and read. Mr Phipps, the forever tolerant foreman, was forever catching me at it.

Talking of graves – one of the poems in this book is called 'Billy McBone'. Was he a real kid?

No. But representative, I hope.

What's the best present you've ever received?

My Christmas pillowcase when I was maybe five or six. I can remember waking up very early, when the house was dark and cold, and opening the door and finding a pillowcase outside. Then dragging it back into bed and examining all the things it contained. That tremendous excitement at getting so many things. We were a pretty poor family but relatively, of course, Christmas is always a time of abundance and excitement in that way, especially when you're young. In those days we didn't just get presents of the usual sort, we'd also get an apple, an orange, some nuts and some sweets. I'd sit awake for hours playing with this stuff. The central, magical bit of the whole thing though, was first opening the bedroom door and in the darkness just seeing the white shape of the pillowcase.

I remember Wiz getting into a pillowcase when he was a kitten. He wriggled about inside it like a little cat-ghost.

Alan Ahlberg

PLEASE MRS BUTLER

Please Mrs Butler
This boy Derek Drew
Keeps copying my work, Miss.
What shall I do?

Go and sit in the hall, dear.
Go and sit in the sink.
Take your books on the roof, my lamb.
Do whatever you think.

Please Mrs Butler
This boy Derek Drew
Keeps taking my rubber, Miss.
What shall I do?

Keep it in your hand, dear.
Hide it up your vest.
Swallow it if you like, my love.
Do what you think best.

Please Mrs Butler
This boy Derek Drew
Keeps calling me rude names, Miss.
What shall I do?

Lock yourself in the cupboard, dear.
Run away to sea.
Do whatever you can, my flower.
But *don't ask me!*

BILLY McBONE

Billy McBone
Had a mind of his own,
Which he mostly kept under his hat.
The teachers all thought
That he couldn't be taught,
But Bill didn't seem to mind that.

Billy McBone
Had a mind of his own,
Which the teachers had searched for for years.
Trying test after test,
They still never guessed
It was hidden between his ears.

Billy McBone
Had a mind of his own,
Which only his friends ever saw.
When the teacher said, 'Bill,
Whereabouts is Brazil?'
He just shuffled and stared at the floor.

Billy McBone
Had a mind of his own,
Which he kept under lock and key.
While the teachers in vain
Tried to burgle his brain,
Bill's thoughts were off wandering free.

COLIN

When you frown at me like that, Colin,
And wave your arm in the air,
I know just what you're going to say:
'Please, Sir, it isn't fair!'

It isn't fair
On the football field
If their team scores a goal.
It isn't fair
In a cricket match
Unless you bat *and* bowl.

When you scowl at me that way, Colin,
And mutter and slam your chair,
I always know what's coming next:
'Please, Sir, it isn't fair!'

It isn't fair
When I give you a job.
It isn't fair when I don't.
If I keep you in
It isn't fair.
If you're told to go out, you won't.

When heads bow low in assembly
And the whole school's saying a prayer,
I can guess what's on your mind, Colin:
'Our Father . . . it isn't fair!'

It wasn't fair
In the Infants.
It isn't fair now.
It won't be fair
At the Comprehensive
(For first years, anyhow).

When your life reaches its end, Colin,
Though I doubt if I'll be there,
I can picture the words on the gravestone now.
They'll say: IT IS NOT FAIR.

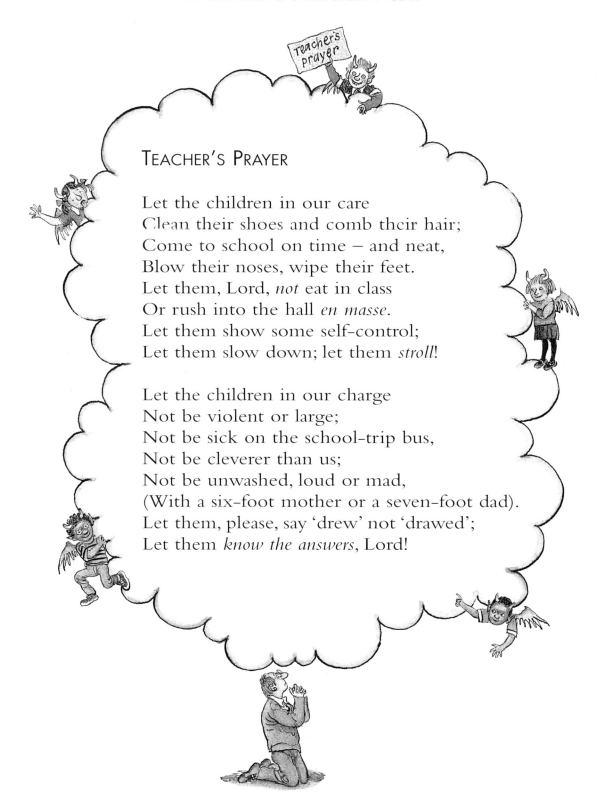

TEACHER'S PRAYER

Let the children in our care
Clean their shoes and comb their hair;
Come to school on time – and neat,
Blow their noses, wipe their feet.
Let them, Lord, *not* eat in class
Or rush into the hall *en masse*.
Let them show some self-control;
Let them slow down; let them *stroll*!

Let the children in our charge
Not be violent or large;
Not be sick on the school-trip bus,
Not be cleverer than us;
Not be unwashed, loud or mad,
(With a six-foot mother or a seven-foot dad).
Let them, please, say 'drew' not 'drawed';
Let them *know the answers*, Lord!

FINISHING OFF

The teacher said:
Come here, Malcolm!
Look at the state of your book.
Stories and pictures unfinished
Wherever I look.

This model you started at Easter,
These plaster casts of your feet,
That graph of the local traffic –
All of them incomplete.

You've a half-baked pot in the kiln room
And a half-eaten cake in your drawer.
You don't even finish the jokes you tell –
I really can't take any more.

And Malcolm said
. . . very little.
He blinked and shuffled his feet.
The sentence he finally started
Remained incomplete.

He gazed for a time at the floorboards;
He stared for a while into space;
With an unlined, unwhiskered expression
On his unfinished face.

BEDTIMF

When I go upstairs to bed,
I usually give a loud cough.
This is to scare The Monster off.

When I come to my room,
I usually slam the door right back.
This is to squash The Man in Black
Who sometimes hides there.

Nor do I walk to the bed,
But usually run and jump instead.
This is to stop The Hand –
Which is under there all right –
From grabbing my ankles.

IT IS A PUZZLE

My friend
Is not my friend any more.
She has secrets from me
And goes about with Tracy Hackett.

I would
Like to get her back,
Only do not want to say so.
So I pretend
To have secrets from her
And go about with Alice Banks.

But what bothers me is,
Maybe *she* is pretending
And would like *me* back,
Only does not want to say so.

In which case
Maybe it bothers her
That *I* am pretending.

But if we are both pretending,
Then really we are friends
And do not know it.

On the other hand,
How can we be friends
And have secrets from each other
And go about with other people?

My friend
Is not my friend any more,
Unless she is pretending.
I cannot think what to do.
It is a puzzle.

THE GHOST TEACHER

The school is closed, the children gone,
But the ghost of a teacher lingers on.
As the daylight fades, as the daytime ends,
As the night draws in and the dark descends,
She stands in the classroom, as clear as glass.
And calls the names of her absent class.

The school is shut, the children grown,
But the ghost of the teacher, all alone,
Puts the date on the board and moves about
(As the night draws on and the stars come out)
Between the desks — a glow in the gloom —
And calls for quiet in the silent room.

The school is a ruin, the children fled,
But the ghost of the teacher, long-time dead,
As the moon comes up and the first owls glide,
Puts on her coat and steps outside.
In the moonlit playground, shadow-free,
She stands on duty with a cup of tea.

The school is forgotten — children forget —
But the ghost of a teacher lingers yet.
As the night creeps up to the edge of the day,
She tidies the Plasticine away;
Counts the scissors — a shimmer of glass —
And says, 'Off you go!' to her absent class.

She utters the words that no one hears,
Picks up her bag . . .
              and
                     disappears.

THINGS I HAVE BEEN DOING LATELY

Things I have been doing lately:
Pretending to go mad
Eating my own cheeks from the inside
Growing taller
Keeping a secret
Keeping a worm in a jar
Keeping a good dream going
Picking a scab on my elbow
Rolling the cat up in a rug
Blowing bubbles in my spit
Making myself dizzy
Holding my breath
Pressing my eyeballs so that I become temporarily blind
Being very nearly ten
Practising my signature . . .

Saving the best till last.

INDEX OF FIRST LINES

Acknowledgements

The publishers gratefully acknowledge permission to reproduce copyright material in this book:

'A Date with Spring', 'Fisherman Chant', 'Spell to Banish a Pimple' and 'The Hurt Boy and the Birds' reprinted from GET BACK, PIMPLE by John Agard (Viking, 1996) copyright © John Agard 1996, 'Hatch Me a Riddle', 'Once Upon a Time', 'Spell to Bring a Smile' and 'The Clown's Last Joke' reprinted from LAUGHTER IS AN EGG by John Agard (Viking, 1990) copyright © John Agard 1990; 'Billy McBone', 'Colin', 'Finishing Off', 'Teacher's Prayer', 'The Ghost Teacher' and 'Things I Have Been Doing Lately' reprinted from HEARD IT IN THE PLAYGROUND by Allan Ahlberg (Viking Kestrel, 1989) copyright © Allan Ahlberg 1989, 'Bedtime', 'It is a Puzzle' and 'Please Mrs Butler' reprinted from PLEASE MRS BUTLER by Allan Ahlberg (Kestrel, 1983) copyright © Allan Ahlberg 1983; 'Janny Jim Jan' and 'My Cat Plumduff' reprinted from EARLY IN THE MORNING by Charles Causley (Viking Kestrel, 1986) copyright © Charles Causley 1986, 'Tell Me, Tell Me, Sarah Jane' from FIGGIE HOBBIN by Charles Causley (Macmillan, 1970) copyright © Charles Causley 1970, 'How to Protect Baby from a Witch', 'I am the Song', 'Mrs McPhee', 'My Mother Saw a Dancing Bear', 'Tam Snow' and 'Who?' from GOING TO THE FAIR by Charles Causley (Viking, 1994) copyright © Charles Causley 1994; 'Brendon Gallacher', 'Names', 'The School Hamster's Holiday' and 'The Want-Want Twins' reprinted from THREE HAS GONE by Jackie Kay (Blackie, 1994) copyright © Jackie Kay 1994, 'I'm Not Old Enough Yet', 'New Baby', 'Pumpkin for Maxine' and 'Waves' reprinted from TWO'S COMPANY by Jackie Kay (Blackie, 1992) copyright © Jackie Kay 1992; 'Elephant' and 'The Reader of This Poem' reprinted from BAD, BAD CATS by Roger McGough (Viking, 1997) copyright © Roger McGough 1997, 'On and on', and 'Strangeways' reprinted from LUCKY by Roger McGough (Viking, 1993) copyright © Roger McGough 1993, 'Love a Duck' reprinted from NAILING A SHADOW by Roger McGough (Viking Kestrel, 1987) copyright © Roger McGough 1987, 'The Sound Collector' reprinted from PILLOW TALK by Roger McGough (Viking, 1990) copyright © Roger McGough 1990, 'Haiku', 'Mrs Moon' and 'Sky in the Pie!' reprinted from SKY IN THE PIE by Roger McGough (Kestrel, 1983) copyright © Roger McGough 1983, 'Gruesome' reprinted from YOU TELL ME by Roger McGough and Michael Rosen (Viking Kestrel, 1979) copyright © Roger McGough 1979; 'Silly Old Baboon' reprinted from A BOOK OF MILLIGANIMALS by Spike Milligan (Dobson Books, 1968) copyright © Spike Milligan Productions Ltd 1985, 'My sister Laura', 'On the Ning Nang Nong', 'Said the General', 'Today I saw a little worm' and 'You must never bath in an Irish Stew' reprinted from SILLY VERSE FOR KIDS by Spike Milligan (Dennis Dobson, 1959, 1961, 1963) copyright © Spike Milligan Productions Ltd 1985, 'A B', 'Kids' and 'Werkling' reprinted from STARTLING VERSE FOR ALL THE FAMILY by Spike Milligan (Michael Joseph, 1987) copyright © Spike Milligan Productions Ltd 1987, 'The Squirdle' and 'The "Veggy" Lion' reprinted from UNSPUN SOCKS FROM A CHICKEN'S LAUNDRY (M & J Hobbs and Michael Joseph, 1981) copyright © Spike Milligan Productions Ltd 1981; 'Looking for Dad', 'Mum Won't Let Me Keep a Rabbit', 'Squeezes', 'The Tree and the Pool' and 'The Whale's Hymn' reprinted from GARGLING WITH JELLY (Viking, 1985) copyright © Brian Patten 1985, 'Don't Forget to Wash Behind Your Hearing-aid', 'Hide-away Sam', 'Rabbit's Spring' and 'The Race to Get to Sleep' reprinted from THAWING FROZEN FROGS by Brian Patten (Viking, 1990) copyright © Brian Patten 1990, 'Uncle Ben from Number One' reprinted from THE UTTER NUTTERS by Brian Patten (Viking, 1994) copyright © Brian Patten 1994; 'Chocolate Cake', 'Shut Your Mouth When You're Eating', 'The Itch', 'Tricks' and 'Unfair' reprinted from QUICK, LET'S GET OUT OF HERE (André Deutsch Ltd, 1983) copyright © Michael Rosen 1983, 'I'm the Youngest in Our House' reprinted from WOULDN'T YOU LIKE TO KNOW (André Deutsch Ltd, 1977) copyright © Michael Rosen 1977, 'Who Started It?' reprinted from YOU WAIT TILL I'M OLDER THAN YOU (Viking, 1996) copyright © Michael Rosen 1996; 'Dave Dirt's Christmas Presents', 'Granny Tom' and 'Mercy' from CAT AMONG THE PIGEONS by Kit Wright (Viking, 1987) copyright © Kit Wright 1987, 'The Man Who Invented Football', 'The Sea in the Trees' and 'Waiting for the Tone' reprinted from GREAT SNAKES by Kit Wright (Viking, 1994) © Kit Wright 1994, 'Greedyguts', 'Song Sung by a Man on a Barge to Another Man on a Different Barge in Order to Drive Him Mad' and 'The Great Detective' reprinted from HOT DOG AND OTHER POEMS by Kit Wright (Kestrel, 1981) copyright © Kit Wright 1981; 'For Word', 'Natural Anthem', 'This Orange Tree' and 'Walking Black Home' reprinted from FUNKY CHICKENS by Benjamin Zephaniah (Viking, 1996) copyright © Benjamin Zephaniah 1996, 'Body Talk', 'Civil Lies', 'Fair Play', 'Luv Song', 'Solidarity' and 'Talking Turkeys!!' reprinted from TALKING TURKEYS by Benjamin Zephaniah (Viking, 1994) copyright © Benjamin Zephaniah 1994.

Every effort has been made to trace copyright holders, but in a few cases this has proved impossible. The editor and publishers apologize for these cases of copyright transgression and would like to hear from any copyright holder not acknowledged.